MW01400324

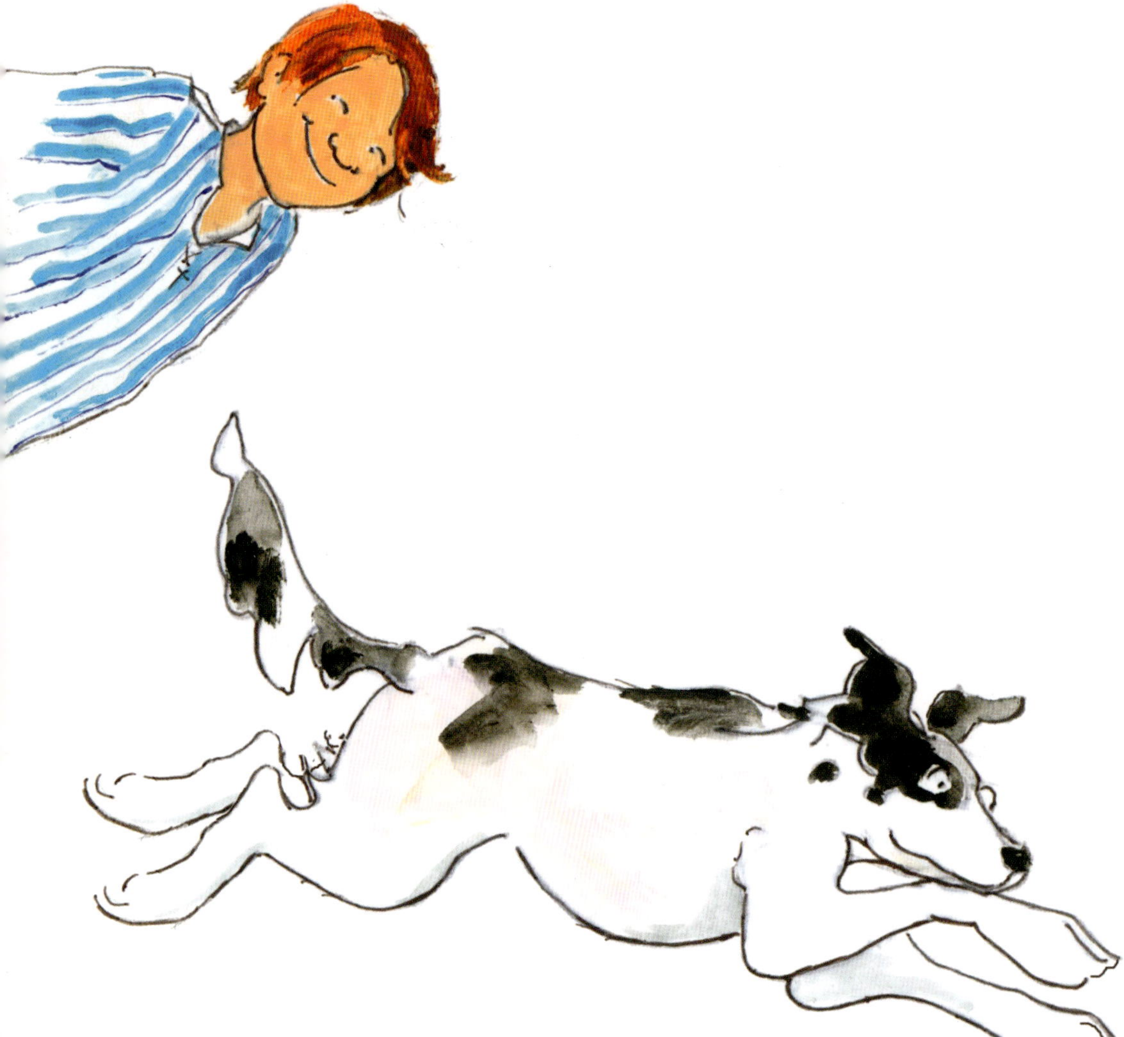

THE FIRST GOOD SHEPHERD

Psalm 23 for Children

Martina Steinkühler
ILLUSTRATED BY Angela Holzmann

Paulist Press
New York / Mahwah, NJ

This is David.
Do you see him sitting?
What is he doing?

Do you see the sheep?
They belong to David's father.
David's father is a rich man.
He has many sheep.
He also has many children.

David is his youngest child.
His father told him to take
the sheep to pasture and
keep them safe.

The sheep are hungry.
The sheep are thirsty.
They like to eat green grass,
and they like to drink fresh water.
David has brought them here
to the green meadow, beside fresh water.

Sheep do not have claws or fangs.
They are not wild, but gentle.
So they fear wild animals like wolves or vultures.
David has a stick, a shepherd's crook,
so that he can scatter wolves and vultures.

Sheep do not like to be alone.
They like to stay together.
But sometimes one gets lost and
does not know the way back.
Then it is very afraid.

David knows all the sheep in his flock. He also knows the youngest one, his favorite. Sometimes he carries it on his shoulders.

Wait! What do you see?
Look closely!
The youngest sheep—
it is not there!
David is also looking
and sees the same
thing.
Do you see him stand-
ing, and looking and
looking and looking?

"It's just the youngest,"
you say?
This does not make
David feel better.

David goes off.
He leaves behind the other sheep on the green pastures with fresh water.
"Stay safe!" he says.

The youngest sheep is not below.
David does not know where to look.
So he goes up between the rocks.
Above—do you see?—vultures are circling!

The sun burns.
The rocks are steep.
Not a blade of grass
grows here.
David struggles up
and leans on his
staff.

Yes, here is the youngest sheep, gently saying, "Baaaa!"

Look at David.
What is he doing?

When David comes back to his flock,
they are still safe, and it is evening.

It gets dark quickly. The sheep are resting.
The youngest is with his mother.
David keeps watch.

He thinks of everything that happened.
He is glad it turned out well.

"I have pastured the sheep," he thinks.
"I pastured them in a green meadow.
I led them to fresh water.
I guarded them.
I found the youngest who was lost.
It was afraid, sitting in the dark.
I came with my staff.
And it was all good."
David looks over all of the sheep.
"I am the good shepherd,"
he says, and taking his flute,
he plays a song:
"The Good Shepherd."

The night is dark.
Wolves howl.
They smell the sheep, and sneak up,
with claws and teeth…
David—are you sleeping?

David wakes up.
He guards his sheep.
He grabs his staff.
Do you see him?
Can you see his face?
David is worried.

He takes a piece of wood
and his staff.
He thinks about his sheep.
"Go away, wolves,
get away from my sheep!
I am the good shepherd!"

Then the wolves are gone.

David sits down.
That's just as well.
His knees are shaking.
Bad things can happen with wolves.

"Bad things can happen with
vultures, too," thinks tired David.
"And in the rocks,
and with the youngest sheep.
All this can also go wrong."

David gets cold.
He looks around.
His sheep are resting peacefully.
And suddenly he wishes
he was one of them
and **he** had a good shepherd.

David plays his song again.
But this time it sounds different.
"Who is my shepherd?" he sings.
"Who brings me to green pastures,
and leads me beside the still waters?
And who really likes me?"

There is David.
It is morning.
The night is over.
The sun rises.
The sheep quietly say, "Baaaa."
They look for fresh pastures.

David drinks the water.
He has baked bread by the fire.
He eats and thinks,
"We have been protected, the sheep and I, all night."

To the Meadow!

For the third time,
David sings his song.
And again
it sounds different:

"The Lord is my shepherd, I shall not want.
    He makes me lie down in green pastures;
he leads me beside the still waters;
    he restores my soul.
He leads me in right paths
    for his name's sake.

Even though I walk through the darkest valley,
    I fear no evil;
for you are with me;
    your rod and your staff—
        they comfort me.

You prepare a table before me
    in the presence of my enemies;
you anoint my head with oil;
    my cup overflows.

Surely goodness and mercy shall follow me
    all the days of my life,
and I shall dwell in the house of the Lord
    my whole life long."

That is David's song.
It is in the Bible,
and in the hearts of people all over the world.
Even today.

Presentation at 3:00 p.m.

Most people are not shepherds.
But what David felt
in the pasture by the creek
and in the night when the wolves came,
people still feel today.

English translation copyright © 2015 by Paulist Press, Inc.

Originally published as
WIE SCHÖN, DASS DU MICH GEFUNDEN HAST!
© 2013 Schwabenverlag AG, Patmos Verlag, Ostfildern

Cover and interior design: Finken &; Bumiller, Stuttgart

Library of Congress Control Number: 2015935284

ISBN 978-0-8091-6774-6 (hardcover)
ISBN 978-1-58768-510-1 (e-book)

Published by
Paulist Press, Inc.
997 Macarthur Boulevard
Mahwah, New Jersey 07430

Printed and bound in the United States of America
by Versa Press, East Peoria, IL
July 2015